THE

BLIND DATE

Book of Romance

CHRISTY CAMPBELL

LWT

Boxtree

BLIND DATE
WITH CILLA BLACK

Produced in Association with
TALBOT TELEVISION LIMITED 1989

Creative Consultants
GRUNDY INTERNATIONAL

Producer
KEVIN ROAST

First published in 1989 by Boxtree Limited

British Library Cataloguing in Publication Data
Campbell, Christopher, 1951–
    The Blind date book of romance.
    1. Romantic love
    I. Title
    152.4

ISBN 1–85283–272–X

Designed by Roger Kohn
Managing Editor: Anna Selby
Photographers: David Farrell, Simon Farrell,
Tony Russell, Mike Vaughan
Illustrator: János Márffy

When I'm Sad (p10) © Adrian Mitchell
from *The Collected Poems* published by Allison & Busby

Typeset by Falcon Graphic Art Limited
Printed in Italy by Imago Publishing Limited
for Boxtree Limited, 36 Tavistock Street, London WC2E 7PB

CONTENTS

Introduction 4

Introducing Barry and Angela 5

What is this thing
Called Love? 6

Blind Date – the Show Where
It All Happens 12

It Takes Two... 16

The Raw Material 18

The British in Love 22

Romancing the Sloane 24

Sexual Chemistry 26

Where to Meet 30

Etiquette for Romantics 34

The Food of Love 37

Gifts of Love 38

Hearts and Flowers 40

Choc Horror 42

A Whiff of Seduction 44

Which Weepie? 45

True Romance 48

Romance on Wheels 50

Romancing the Bean 52

Going for the Clinch 54

'I Just Called to Say I Love You' 56

Love Hurts 58

Communication Breakdown 60

Happy Ending 62

What is it that has made Blind Date one of Britain's best loved TV shows? It's got to be the Blind Daters themselves.

Show after show, they charm and outrage all of us on both sides of the screen with their mixture of genuineness and irrepressible good humour.

Why it all works of course is that in matters of romance, heartbreak and laughter are always walking hand in hand.

I suppose that's the secret of **Blind Date**. All the world loves a lover, and romance is what makes the world go round. So, what London Weekend Television decided the world needed was a guide to the whole business of falling in (and out) of love. And where better to start than with **Blind Date** – the show where it all happens?

So here it is — **The Blind Date Book of Romance** — the chat-ups, the put-downs, the dream dates and the disasters.

A lorra lorra luv'

Cilla
xx

INTRODUCING BARRY 'N' ANGELA

Hi! My name's Barry and I'm from London. Well, that's how the lads do the old 'my name's Bond' routine on Blind Date — so it should do nicely by way of an introduction to *The Blind Date Book of Romance*. You see, those clever people at London Weekend Television decided that what the world really needed was a survival guide to the painful business of falling in and falling out of love.

And where better to start than the show where sexual chemistry really seems to fizz and bubble — if you really want to know why people are attracted to each other (and why in the game of romance some of us make such terrible mistakes) — the Blind Date studio is the perfect place.

You see, I'm having this thing with Angela who works in the Blind Date office — well I'm trying to have this thing with Angela. I love her, I really do . . . and I know she finds me attractive — well, all the girls do really.

But Angela and I can't quite seem to get our act together. I mean, I do everything I can to make her happy, I take her to movies, I send her flowers, we go for romantic walks on windswept beaches . . . but Angela just goes all mopey and won't **commit** herself. She's not ready, she says, our relationship is too grown-up to clutter it up with all that gooey hand-holding. But I don't want friendship — I want love!

So the Blind Date people asked me to keep a diary of life at the sharp end of love's young dream and file my reports from the front line of romance — all I can say is that I hope it gives some other poor bloke out there a clue . . .

Hello — I'm Angela and I'm from Surrey. As if life in the Blind Date office wasn't busy enough, now I've been asked to keep a diary of my love life. They want to use it in some silly book.

What love life? I'm potty about this guy Barry but he just doesn't seem to notice. It's been . . . how long now? . . . six months since we met at that awful party. He was so nice, he rang the next day just as he promised he would. He's taken me out, we've even been away for the weekend together — but he just won't make a move. He just goes all soppy and wants to hold hands — and nothing else! God, I hate wimps, don't you? But Barry's not like that really, I know one day he'll just go for it, out of the blue, tell me he loves me — he might even give me a kiss.

So girls, if everything's a bit iffy in the romance department, I hope my little problems will go to show there's a lot of us out there . . .

You may think life is speeding you by . . . but it's never too late to fall in love

WHAT IS THIS THING CALLED LOVE?

WHAT THE SCIENTISTS SAY

When the going gets romantic, the romantic gets going

People have been trying to define this thing called love since one amoeba eyed up another amoeba in some primeval slime and decided that life as a creature that reproduced by simply splitting in two was getting a bit boring. Sexual attraction, call it lust if you like, would seem sufficient to ensure the human race continued to reproduce itself — so why do we mess things up by falling in love?

The A-Z of Psychology gives Romantic Love short shrift — 'Romantic passion may be a good foundation for short-lived sexual relationships,' it says, 'but by its very nature romance is brief and passion founded on it quickly wanes.' So don't say we didn't warn you.

Veteran ape-watcher Desmond Morris has some very shrewd notions of what

love is all about, based on many years of watching both naked and hairy apes in action. First of all, us lot — *homo sapiens*. We are very different from other primates. Did you know, for example, that monkeys do not form deep bonds of attachment with their mates and that they indulge in very little courtship behaviour before they get down to it? 'The whole encounter is usually over in a few seconds,' says Morris.

Just like some men, you might say, but the big buzz-word in human behaviour is pair-bonding, the creation of a strong and stable unit of two adults who will conjoin, not just for the process of reproduction but who will stay together through the long and complex business of raising a human child.

And teddy came too . . . They say you revert to babyhood when you fall in love — but this is ridiculous

It is love that makes it all possible, but love is notoriously fickle and elusive — so we have invented marriage as a kind of superglue to stick us all together.

Morris also has a fascinating answer to why lovers get sloppier and sloppier as romance progresses. 'From where do humans derive all the gentle, hesitant touchings and hand-holdings of human courtship? In terms of the behaviour involved, falling in love looks like a return to infancy.' Try this theory for size —

Step 1 A couple meet — they interact formally as any new acquaintances might. They behave as socially conditioned adults and talk about adult concerns. They are normal grown-ups.

Step 2 They begin to get interested in each other — and begin a voyage **backward** in time. They walk hand in hand as each once did with a parent.

Step 3 They travel even further back in time. Their intimate caresses are like those of a mother towards a newborn baby.

Step 4 At last they are naked — 'and for the first time since they were tiny babies, the most private parts of their bodies experience the intimate touch of another's hands,' Morris explains.

Step 5 Even speech patterns dissolve into goo-goo, diddums, darling bunnikins etc, etc, ad nauseam. They have become babbling infants.

So you see, it's perfectly simple — falling in love is nothing to do with becoming more grown up, it's about becoming a baby all over again. This is why Valentine small-ads placed by otherwise perfectly rational grown-ups carry such messages as 'Baby Bear loves Poo-Poo Bum'. That is why lovers give each other as presents not food mixers or calculators but cuddly toys and gooey chocolates. So next time you have a romantic assignation, forget candlelight and roses — just nip down to Mothercare and grab a couple of giant-sized Babygros. Here is a real Valentine's message from the *The Times* — see what we mean . . . ?

TO DEBBIE Pookie People Pips from Petey Popsy Pooples — I Love you — be mine.

... AND SOME MORE THEORIES

The Love Scale

American psychologist Zick Rubin devised a scale against which love can be measured. It has three main degrees —

* Attachment — wanting to be with the other person and giving and receiving emotional support
* Caring — genuine and deep concern and a feeling of responsibility for the other partner
* Intimacy — the close and confidential sharing of thoughts and feelings with each other

When all these occur **together** and are felt by both partners, then a couple is in love. While they may both be 'attached' and 'caring' — showing respect and admiration for each other — but have not progressed to intimacy, they are merely 'in like' with each other.

— or these, 'Let's dance cheek to cheek' perhaps?

Body language may say it all – but what are these Blind Daters trying to say?

Love Knots — Those Giveaway Signs

As well as the more obvious signals such as holding hands, embracing and kissing, a couple in love will exhibit 'tie-signs'. For instance, they will
*spend a good deal of time just staring into each other's eyes
*stand close together and turn their bodies inwards to exclude outsiders
*avoid conversation with other people and speak to each other in low whispers
*indulge in baby-talk, cuddling and general yucky gooiness
*Couples in love also tend to move in the same or similar way and make these movements at the same time, mirroring each other's gestures, sitting or standing in similar postures even — smiling and moving their heads simultaneously.

Ten Completely Useless Facts You Probably Never Wanted To Know About Love

1 Once upon a time in Korea, marriage based upon love was illegal.

2 In many Asian cultures to show affection publicly is regarded as the absolute height of bad manners.

3 The average human being of modern times can expect to enjoy half a century of active sexual life, matched among mammals only by whales and elephants.

4 The average male baboon gets through both courtship and mating in record time — less than 10 seconds.

5 In some South Pacific island cultures, romance is completely unknown. They regard 'sexual pleasure as the result of adept technical performance engaged in by individuals who experience transitory attraction for each other'.

6 In villages in Pakistan, a bridegroom-to-be is brought before the bride's family and subjected to a barrage of insults about his manhood — so he has nothing to fear from what his bride will say later.

7 Around the world, more than 900 substances regarded as aphrodisiacs have been recorded including asparagus, caviar, eel, garlic, ginseng, honey, lobster, oysters, pearls and truffles. Giacomo Casanova ate fifty oysters for breakfast every day.

8 A love-spell practised in the West Indies by a woman who wants to make a man take notice of her is to boil her knickers in a pot and use the water to make a drink for the man she has her eye on . . .

9 The famous Kinsey report on human sexuality published in the US in the late 1940s recorded the case of an anonymous American who claimed to have made love to his partner five times a day for 30 years. However, Kinsey calculated the average frequency for an American male's sexual activity (from puberty to old age) to be 2.3 times per week.

10 Research in Australia has shown that kissing can spread tooth decay — and that the merest peck can raise the normal heart-rate from 72 to 95 beats per second — enough, says one American scientist, to knock 17 seconds off our lives each time we kiss.

'**Love** — a form of mental illness not yet recognised in any of the standard diagnostic manuals'

Macmillan Dictionary of Psychology

Casanova thought oysters were the perfect aphrodisiac. This Blind Dater obviously has her own ideas

If the scientists fail hopelessly to define what love is, then there's no shortage of poets, lyricists, singers, playwrights and song writers — not to mention out-and-out cynics — to give us a clue. This is Oscar Wilde's definition of romance —

When one is in love one always begins by deceiving oneself, and one always ends by deceiving others. That is what the world calls a romance.

WHAT THE POETS SAY

Oscar had his own problems but not everyone is quite so cynical. Geoffrey Chaucer wrote this about love six hundred years ago —

Thus in heaven he took
    his delight,
And smothered her with
    kisses upon kisses
Till gradually he came to
    learn where bliss is
    Troilus and Criseyde

And here's a simple cheery-up making thought from a modern poet, Adrian Mitchell —

When I'm sad and
    weary,
When I think all hope is
    gone.
When I walk along High
    Holborn,
I think of you with
    nothing on.
        When I'm Sad

And Woody Allen's views about how a love affair has to be continually worked at —

A relationship, I think, is like a shark. You know? It has to constantly move forward or it dies.
        Annie Hall

But it's not just the blissful course of true and enduring love that makes poets snatch up their pens. The cruel muse of betrayal and heartbreak is just as deep a source of inspiration.

Shakespeare spoke a universal truth one in of his *Sonnets* —

When my Love swears
    she is made of truth.
I do believe her, though
    I know she lies.
        Sonnet 138

And the nineteenth-century poet Swinburne knew how love could grow cold.

I remember the way we
    parted,
    The day and the way
    we met;
You hoped we were
    both broken hearted,
    And knew we should
    both forget.
And the best and the
    worst of this is,
    That neither is most
    to blame,
If you have forgotten
    my kisses,
    And I have forgotten
    your name.

A relationship is like a shark — well, sometimes

Romance can be a magic carpet ride

the magic carpet
FLY AROUND THE WORLD WITH AUROMAXEV

But however bruising poets may find the process of falling out of love, they always seem ready to come back for more. Lord Byron (who was reputed to have had three hundred love affairs) offered us this pearl of wisdom on the nature of woman —

In her first passion a
    woman loves her lover,
    In all the others all she
    loves is love.
                Don Juan

And some men who would not necessarily profess to be poets have waxed quite lyrical. There's this view of women from Aristotle Onassis, a man who had both a lot of money and a lot of women —

If women didn't exist, all the money in the world would have no meaning.

Groucho Marx had this to say —

Anyone who says he can see through a woman is missing a lot.

And here are some views of men from three ladies who should know a thing or two about the subject —

Give a man a free hand and he'll run it all over you.
                Mae West

Macho does not prove mucho.
                Zsa Zsa Gabor

The average man is more interested in a woman who is interested in him than he is in a woman with beautiful legs.
                Marlene Dietrich

BLIND DATE

THE SHOW WHERE IT ALL HAPPENS

Here on Blind Date of course we know everything there is to know about romance. We don't need all those psychologists to tell us about the mysteries of human attraction — it happens right here, week by week, as our pickers and pickees shape up for that first encounter . . . and in the second part of the game, when our Blind Daters return from their day of destiny — some with tales of happiness and laughter, some with tales of affection spurned and some with tales of all-out unarmed combat which would make a sumo wrestling match look tame!

First Impressions

They say first impressions are important, and when that screen goes back the picker gets to meet the pickees — the lucky winner and the ones that got away. Sometimes they are not quite what they were expecting. Try these first impressions from satisfied and not-so-satisfied customers —

Her 'When the screen pulled back I nearly died of fright.'   – Helen about Mark

Her 'I was expecting this tall dark handsome fella. Well, he was certainly dark, tall — but not so much of the other.'
                    – Susanne about Jason

Him 'I was faced with this dark-haired, green-eyed beauty.'
                    – Mark about Helen

Her 'I thought he'd be tall and dashing and he was actually quite large and relatively ugly.'
                    – Helen about Mark

Him 'My first reaction was just of this hair coming towards me.'
                    – Rob about Julie

Him 'The screen went back and there was an apparition of . . . mmm . . . fairly good beauty.'
                    – Mark about Becky

Her 'I thought he was going to be really macho — I was expecting a really hunky guy — but when I saw him, I thought, what a wimp.'
                    – Julie about Rob

Him 'I was quite surprised at her make-up . . . it was a bit over the top — I thought of directing her to the burns department.'
                    – Jason about Susanne

The Things They Say

After The Date comes the reckoning. A couple of days after their time spent together in some exotic locale, they come back to the studio and we ask them to tell us just how they got on. It's a bit like de-briefing a bomber crew who have flown deep behind enemy lines — and sometimes there's been just as much flak!

First of all there are the couples who seem to have been on dates with completely different people —

A line-up of pickees . . .

Celebrating Christmas with Cilla

Keeping an eye on developments

WERE THEY ON THE SAME DATE TOGETHER?

Bruno and Kate

Him 'I think she liked me — no, I **know**.'

Her 'Then he lost his passport which was quite good because hopefully he'd have to stay on the plane till I got back.'

Mark and Helen

Her 'His problem with canoeing was that he didn't have a clue — he fell in about seven times.'

Him 'I fell in once.'

Clare and Andrew

Her 'He's a very Mills & Boon person.'

Him 'If I was compared to a character in Mills & Boon I'd die on the spot —'

Darren and Gabby

Him 'We certainly were impressed with each other.'

Her 'Speak for yourself . . .

Lorraine and Steve

Him 'I like to think of myself as quite good-looking and witty.'

Her 'I would definitely describe him as a male chauvinist pig . . . as well as a prat, an idiot and a wally.'

Cath and Paul

Her 'He was wearing this stone-washed denim jacket which I really didn't like at all.'

Him 'I think she liked the way I was dressed.'

Steve and Susan

Him 'When I was with her I only had eyes for her — I never looked at ânyone else.'

Her 'Every time a leggy blonde went walking past he'd turn his head.'

Barbie and Nigel

Her 'We are completely different, like chalk and cheese in more or less every aspect.'

Him 'I thought we were very compatible . . . we had a lot of things in common and were very much alike.'

Him 'We both had the same warped kind of sense of humour and laughed a lot.'

Her 'I didn't find his jokes very funny . . .'

Then there are those who don't want to say anything **really nasty** about their date. Perhaps it's even worse when they indulge in a little bit of —

DAMNING WITH FAINT PRAISE

Her 'I would describe him as an average sort of person, not wacky but not boring — you know like a ham salad.'

Sharon about James

Him 'I would say she was small, petite, you know . . . dinky.'

Steve about Susan

Him 'I liked her hair even if there was lots of peroxide in it.'

Paul about Cath

Him 'I think Maria's best quality was mmmm . . . mmmm . . . mmmm.'

David about Maria

Him 'I think she'd end up marrying someone from the royal family.'

Andrew about Clare

Her 'We had quite a lot in common — we're both allergic to cats.'

Julie about Senna

Him 'If she phoned me up I'd probably say yes . . .'

Jason about Susanne

And there are those Blind Daters who find that, although things might have all gone swimmingly in the studio, a little time spent in each other's company proved that, right from the start, they were —

Mr and Mrs Wrong for each other . . .

Maria and David

Her 'The highlight was when he nearly got run over by a bike in the Amsterdam flower auction.'

Him 'The only bit of contact we had during the whole day was when I tried to throw her into one of the canals.'

Andrew and Clare

Him 'Asked whether I'd see her again I'd say — yes, I might keep in touch.'

Her 'Marry me . . . !?!'

Nick and Marie

Him 'We started dancing together — I went to the toilet and when I came back she was dancing with this Italian fella —'

Her 'Nick had the

feeling he was being ditched, but he wasn't . . . he was just being boring —'

Him 'I think if we'd been in Sicily for more than a week, I'd have taken Marie up Mount Etna and thrown her in.'

Him 'I think the ideal place for her would maybe be a padded cell, that way she wouldn't get to upset anyone.'

Iffy romances

Him 'We were a bit iffy in the romance department.'

James about Sharon

Him 'She was a lot older than me . . . she was 24 and I was 23.'

David about Maria

Her 'It's the usual problem — Londoners can't speak right.'

Elissa about David

Her 'He only had eyes for the horse.'

Helen about Mark

Him 'If I could change one thing about her — it would have to be her right hook . . .'

Kevin about Anna

Her 'He made me laugh, and I think I made him

laugh too . . . actually I think he was laughing quite a lot at me.'

Suzanne about Jason

Adrian and Tania

Him 'She seemed to enjoy talking to herself — which was quite a relief for the rest of us.'

Her 'How would you feel about someone you've spent a wonderful day with, had a fabulous champagne lunch with — who then says you're fat?'

Then there are the ones who, after spending only a little while in each other's company realise that, even on Blind Date, they can make a **ghastly mistake**. That's when we get to all-out war and the gentle art of —

The perfect putdown!

Him 'Her ideal date would be someone older than her . . . who looks like Jasper Carrot.'

David about Maria

Him 'The thing I liked about her most was her feet.'

Paul about Elenia

Him 'What was the most romantic thing in the day? Coming home.'

John about Melanie

Him 'The best thing about her is her sense of humour — that's the only good thing about her.'

John about Melanie

Him 'Yes I was almost asleep on that interview then . . . I suppose I must have been thinking about her.'

John about Melanie

Her 'If he turned up at work . . . I'd hope that he hadn't seen me and get someone to say I was off sick.'

Gabby about Darren

Him 'She'd be good as a girlfriend to come and talk to . . . about your girlfriend.'

Nick about Alyson

Anna and Kevin

Him 'I did say she looked like a model — OK, so it was a model aircraft.'

Her 'I think he'd make a very nice boyfriend . . . for somebody.'

Ricky and Clare

Him 'If I had to compare her to an animal it would be the Black Rhino — there was definitely a resemblance.'

Her 'I'd compare him to a hyena — he was laughing all the time.'

Then there are those really sad ones — which get the audience going with some heartfelt aaaahs . . . and even a few boooooos!!! — where one of the couple is **smitten** but the other definitely is **not**! It all goes to show that —

Love Hurts

Him 'Anna is a lovely girl . . . but I think she deserves someone better than me.'

Kevin about Anna

Her 'I really liked him . . . I don't know what I did wrong.'

Julie about Rob

Him 'I think for Josephine to fall in love with me, I'd have to go in for enormous facial surgery.'

Russell about Josephine

Him 'The one thing I regret was that I would like to have kissed her as she got out of the car — but she was out before I could do it.'

Mark about Helen

Him 'You come to terms with rejection eventually.'

Paul about Clare

Him 'It was a Cinderella kind of day and it's gone and at the same time I really did want to see her — but she didn't leave me a glass slipper.'

Russell about Josephine

Dream Dates Do Come True!

But it's not all warfare — believe us! Some of our Blind Daters have a really smashing time and the nicest things to say about each other when they come back . . .

'She's a lovely woman, I made the right choice — I'd love to meet her again, she's truly part of me.'

Bert about Grace

'Andrew was my ideal Blind Date — he's very charming, very attractive — he's the perfect gentleman.'

Claire about Andrew

'He's a real gentleman, very kind, thoughtful, funny . . . a very sensitive person. I can imagine him getting hurt easily in a relationship — which I would never do to him.'

Julie about Senar

Him 'I couldn't have asked for a better date — she really made it.'

Senar about Julie

Her 'He's not the sort of person to make my knees wobble and my heart miss a beat — but I'd like to know him for the rest of my life.'

Julie about Senar

'I'd walk a million miles to be near her.'

Drew about Nina

And Things They Wish They'd Never Said

Her 'When Jeff was playing golf one of his balls exploded . . .'

Tina about Jeff

IT TAKES TWO...

A lot of romantic poetry, it seems, is written by men wimping on about just what little heart-breakers women are. It was ever thus, but such outpourings are important evidence in answering that age-old question —

Who's More Romantic — Men or Women?
Believe it or not, in survey after survey, **men** show up as being more vulnerable and compulsive than women in matters of love. Men are more likely to commit suicide after a broken love affair (although women attempt it more often) and respond angrily and aggressively to betrayal whereas women will tend to internalise their grief.

But girls start having romantic experiences earlier than boys and have more of them — until, that is, the age of 20. But as soon as **marriage** appears on the horizon, young women seem to get all practical and pushy — while men drift on being sloppy and romantic.

Personal column
In an extensive analysis of personal ads placed in newspapers and magazines by single British men and women looking for partners, researchers found that —
* Women offer good looks and genuineness
* If women are young, they mention it
* Women tend to look for older partners
* Men want attractive women who are younger than themselves
* Men offer money and status

A big survey of more than 1000 boy and girl college students aged between 18 and 24 showed that the average age for a first 'infatuation' for a girl was 13, for a boy it was six months later. Girls typically had their first experience of love at 17, again boys were six months behind. Overall, girls declared a greater number of infatuations than boys and were more likely to have experienced falling in love.

But come the age of 20, the girls get down to being **serious** — the number of new romantic encounters they're after begins to drop off. Men, on the other hand, are still hunting for love.

Scientists interpreted these results as implying that, as women enter their early twenties, they are looking for a marriage partner to whom they can and will be faithful. Previous lovers and surplus present lovers are consciously or unconsciously rejected because they conflict with this ideal. As they mature, therefore, women become more rational and grown-up about their romantic inclinations — while men just carry on as before. Told you so . . .

Well, down to the basic ingredients of romance — boys and girls, men and women, oldies and golden goodies —

You're never too old to fall in love

Young love. And you can guarantee there'll be a lot of fooling around until things start to get a little more serious —

— like making a splash in the pool

What could be more romantic than a walk in the rain?

THE RAW MATERIAL
THE BRITISH MALE

There are 26.9 million men in Britain. 3.5 million are aged 0-9, 4.0 million are aged 10-19, 8.3 million aged 20-39, 6.2 million aged 40-59, 3.6 million aged 60-74 and 1.2 million aged 75 and over. 65.7% of them are married, 3.1% divorced, 3.6% widowed and 27.6% single.

The British male is an interesting specimen and comes in all shapes and sizes. . .

What Do They Get up To?

In a recent government poll of British men aged between 20 and 44, the percentages of those who had carried out various activities in the month before they were questioned were —

	Age		
	20-24	25-29	30-44
Going out for a drink	89%	84%	73%
Watching television	99%	98%	99%
DIY		43%	61%	67%
Reading books	48%	51%	55%
Needlework/knitting	3%	4%	3%

What Do They Think About Themselves?

*88% of British men think of themselves as attractive

*6% of British men think of themselves as very attractive

*6% of British men think of themselves as not attractive

*To be attractive to women, men think they have to have —

a. A muscular chest and shoulders

b. Large biceps

c. A large penis

. . . and who can possibly say just what qualities make up the perfect man?

The Ideal Man, The Perfect Woman

In a wide scale survey conducted in the US and Northern Europe, those questioned were asked to express their preferences in facial beauty. The most popular mix of features for both men and women was —

* An oval shaped face
* Large eyes, preferably blue in colour
* Long eyelashes
* Nose straight in profile with a diamond shaped front
* Mouth neither too long nor too narrow
* The distance from mouth to chin should be less than the height of the forehead

You might find the athletic type most appealing and go for him. . .

there again, there is the guy who looks as if he really knows where he's going

. . .or, if you like a little life in your man, try someone who might jump in any direction

Ten Things You Probably Didn't Know About British Men

★ The average British man's brain is 10% heavier than the average woman's

★ Men are three times more likely to commit suicide over a broken love affair than women (although women attempt it more often)

★ Men tend to be attracted to a woman initially by looks rather than personality

★ It has often been quoted that one British man in 10 is exclusively gay — although recent research points to a lower figure

★ 39% of British men are overweight

★ 3% of British males are virgins on their wedding night

★ Men between the ages of 16 and 24 think about sex on average every eight minutes

★ Men reach their sexual peak at 16

★ Three out of 10 British husbands are having affairs

★ The majority of men claim they notice a woman's eyes before any other part of her body

★ 30% of British men express an enjoyment of love making in the living room, 16% in a car, 11% in the kitchen

What Do Men Prefer in Women?

According to a large-scale poll run by Britain's leading computer dating agency, as far as British males are concerned, the perfect woman is — single, has an average build rather than slim, has no political views, is of average attractiveness and has had an average sort of education.

The least wanted woman in Britain is — separated, has a posh accent, is heavily built, unattractive, smokes and drinks.

The British Female

Blue-eyed, blonde
and beautiful

There are 26.9 million women in Britain. 3.5 million are aged 0-9, 4.0 million are aged 10-19, 8.3 million aged 20-39, 6.2 million aged 40-59, 3.6 million aged 60-74 and 1.2 million aged 75 and over. 65.7% of them are married, 3.1% divorced, 3.6% widowed and 27.6% are single.

What Do They Get Up To?

In a government poll of British women between 20-44 these percentages carried out various activities in the months before they were questioned —

	Age		
	20-24	25-29	30-44
Going out for a drink	86%	65%	58%
Watching television	99%	99%	99%
DIY	28%	37%	38%
Reading books	64%	65%	67%
Needlework/knitting	40%	46%	52%

What Do They Think of Themselves?

* 88% of British women think they are attractive
* 10% of British women think of themselves as very attractive
* 2% of British women think they are not attractive
* One in 10 British women believes herself to be an excellent lover

And Things You Probably Didn't Know About British Women

* The average British woman is 5ft 3½in and weighs 134 lb
* Women reach their sexual peak aged between 30 and 35
* Women enjoy their wedding day more than men
* Women respond better than men to stress
* Women are more likely to respond to betrayal by their partner by displaying depression rather than anger
* Women are more faithful than men
* Most women express a preference for a dominant partner
* 4% of British women aged under 45 make love seven times a week
* 49% of British women aged under 45 make love once a week
* 46% of British women expressed an enjoyment for love making in the living room, 4% in the kitchen
* Women notice men's bottoms more than any other feature
* When shown in advertising, women are three times more likely than men to be depicted fulfilling domestic functions inside the house

Well, what do women prefer in men?

What could be nicer raw material for romance than this?

or this. . . .

What Do Women Prefer in Men?

While men think, in physical terms, that they have to be all hairy and muscular to be attractive to women, when women are asked what **they** like, all that macho beefcake is actually a turn-off. When asked to choose what they really go for, it's a tall, slim physique and small buttocks.

A big dating agency survey found that as far as British women are concerned, the perfect man is —
* Single, of average build, never smokes, drinks occasionally, has a degree, went to grammar school, is Church of England and has no interest in politics. He is 'attractive' rather than 'very attractive'.

Britain's least wanted man is —
* A beer-bellied, irreligious, ill-educated, smoking socialist.

So that's the raw material, quite promising really: tinkers, tailors, soldiers, sailors, butchers, bakers and candlestick makers — rich girls, poor girls, air hostesses, beauticians, lawyers, doctors — Sloanes, yuppies, punks . . . and estate agents. But what happens when we all get down to it? Next we ask the question — *How romantic are the British . . . ?*

THE BRITISH IN LOVE
THE FACTS

All the world loves a lover, they say, and there is a whole world of romance for lovers to explore. A woman or a man looking for a partner has two thousand million possible mates in the world to choose from. A love-hungry woman has a slight advantage — there ae 1006 males in the world for every 1000 females. The country with the biggest shortage of males is the Soviet Union, where there are 132 extra females for every 1000 males. In Pakistan, by contrast, for every 1000 males there is a shortage of 94 women.

But as yet there is no dating agency specialising in long-haul romance — introducing rugby-playing, non-smoking, solvent, Porsche-driving Eskimos, for example, to cinema-loving, shy, sincere Japanese ladies. No, as ever, the girl or boy we fall for tends to be the girl or boy next door . . .

In Britain, the overwhelming majority of married couples are born within 10 miles of each other. And four out of five married couples in Britain choose someone of the same race, the same level of parental income, the same religion and same level of intelligence.

Does all this sound a bit samey? The British may not have a world class reputation for being in the first division of red-hot romantics, but our rainy little island has produced more than its share of torrid love affairs, from Lancelot and Guinevere to Nelson and Lady Hamilton.

How Romantic are the British? Did You Know—

* that Britain is a good place for a chap looking for romance because there are more women than men. For every 1000 males there are 1053 females, but the surplus is slowly dropping: by the year 2000 there will be only 35 extra females for every 1000 males
* that 30% of British couples meet their eventual marriage partner at discos, dances and parties
* that when *True Romance* magazine polled its 1.2 million women readers to discover what they really yearned for, the top choice for a romantic location was a wonderful evening sipping champagne on a deserted tropical island with the man of their dreams — as the sun sank slowly in the west. Four out of every 10 readers wished their lovers would be **more** romantic, two-thirds expressed a burning desire to be married with children.

And if what we do on Valentine's Day is anything to go by, then the British are certainly getting more and more romantic — as these amazing facts reveal . . .

* Valentine's Day is the highest male card-buying occasion of the year — the heaviest spenders are men aged 16-30.
* The British send a staggering 16 million Valentine cards every year
* Microbiology student Bruce Ferguson of Rugby gave his wife Helen a card made from 500 billion bacteria he had grown to form the words 'I Love You'

The British in love – we can wear our hearts on our sleeves – or on our heads when we feel like it . . .

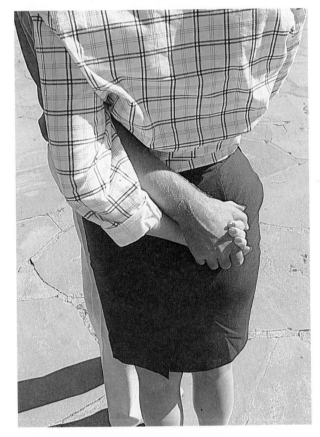

. . . or be ever so discreet

Great British Romantics — Lancelot and Guinevere

From the age of chivalry, when pursuing the favour of a fair damsel came second only to pursuing the Holy Grail, this tale of forbidden love really made the Kingdom swing. As legend tells it, the beautiful Guinevere was King Arthur's Queen, but bored by having to polish the round table every day, she fell for Lancelot, the knight in shining armour whom she certainly found bedazzling.

When their chivalrous moping around turned to something more passionate, Arthur went potty and poor Guinevere paid for her passion with her life.

Robin Hood and Maid Marian

A man with more arrows than Cupid's in his quiver, when he wasn't busy riding through the glen, Robin Hood was laying siege to the heart of Maid Marian. But the beastly Sheriff of Nottingham had his own thoughts on the matter. Perhaps Robin was spending too much time with the merry men . . . nevertheless a fine British romance.

Nelson and Lady Hamilton

When Britain's greatest naval hero wasn't sweeping the French from the seas he was sweeping the beautiful Lady Emma Hamilton off her feet. The trouble was she was already married, to the British consul in Naples, where Nelson's man 'o' war was conveniently berthed. But Sir William Hamilton, the compliant consul, had to turn his own blind eye on Horatio and Emma's carryings on, while Lady Nelson had to grin and bear it at home – after all the amorous admiral would soon have a whole column of his own to remind the nation of his martial prowess.

ROMANCING THE SLOANE

THE ROYALS AND ROMANCE

If the only games you associate with the Kings and Queens of England are polo and charades you couldn't be more wrong. Didn't you know they have been playing Royal Blind Date since the Middle Ages?

It went like this. All those princes and princesses had to be married off — to someone suitable like another prince or princess. Little matter that the betrothed couple might have no interest in each other whatsoever. What mattered was that dynasties should continue and foreign alliances be sealed. And so they played Blind Date, merrily sending portraits and poetry until the match was made.

The trouble was the matches were not always made in heaven and, unlike our own pickers and pickees, there could be a whole **reign** to sit out in grumpy mutual loathing.

Never mind, being royal had its compensations, as you can find out in our —

Blind Date Guide to Royals in Love

Elizabeth I, the Virgin Queen, insisted throughout her reign that she was the most beautiful and desirable woman in the kingdom — it went with the job. She had a stream of suitors who seemed to agree with her, including Sir Walter Ralegh who founded the colony of Virginia as a kind of giant Valentine's card, and her last lover the Earl of Essex. He was an ardent swain in spite of being a quarter of a century her junior — but he ended up being beheaded for treachery.

King Charles II was **deeply** romantic; in fact, pursuing women was his favourite pursuit. He earned his nickname 'Old Rowley' by supposedly equalling the romantic feats and stamina of a goat of that name, kept tethered on the palace green.

While his future kingdom was under the Puritan grip of Oliver Cromwell, Charles roamed Europe, flitting from the bedrooms of pretty aristocratic lady to pretty aristocratic lady, producing a vast number of children as a result. As king, Charles continued to pursue his hobby, having his pick of court beauties — and beauties who just happened to catch his eye like Nell Gwyn, the London actress and orange seller, who joined the stable of regal favourites in 1669.

Meanwhile his Queen Catherine learned not to complain at the number of mistresses he had, nor at the open acceptance she was expected to show them. Catherine never produced an heir.

George II also had innumerable mistresses. He showed a kind of sincerity in his affection for his queen, Caroline, when she, on her death-bed, begged him to re-marry. 'No,' he sobbed, 'I shall only have mistresses.'

George III, unlike the rest of the Hanoverians, **was** faithful to his wife but, to keep his younger brothers and sons in check he forced through the Royal Marriages Act of 1772 which made marriage by a member of the royal family valid only with the king's permission.

His eldest son, the Prince of Wales and future king **George IV** actually married Maria Fitzherbert in secret but the Act allowed him to dump her unceremoniously and look for a royal princess to share his Pavilion in Brighton.

George's unlucky choice was Caroline of Brunswick. He got so drunk on his wedding day that he spent his wedding night in a stupor on the bedroom floor and Queen Caroline was locked out of her own coronation. George was romantic enough, however, to wear a locket containing a miniature portrait of Mrs Fitzherbert until the day he died.

King Edward VIII, 'David' to his friends, gave up the throne for the woman he loved. In earlier days the King might have made a marriage of convenience and kept his love for Mrs Wallis Simpson a royal secret, but times had changed and the most famous royal romance of the twentieth century was the result. His insistence on marrying the American divorcée brought down on him the wrath of the Government and the Church. In 1936 the King was forced to abdicate in order, as he explained in the famous radio broadcast to the nation, that he might marry 'the woman I love'.

And after all that, as we all know, the royal family became **utterly** respectable.

Queen for a day

But watch out . . . royal romances could be a short-lived affair, as Henry VIII's wives found out

Royal Lonely Hearts

Henry VIII married his third wife, Anne of Cleves, on the strength of a Blind Date. A beautiful portrait of her by the court painter Holbein was presented to the King, and Henry's heart was won. But when he clapped eyes on her he was horrified, dubbing the dumpy Anne 'The Flanders Mare'. Perhaps he would have done better to have tried the lonely hearts columns — like this . . .

TALL, COSMOPOLITAN MALE, Own business, several luxury homes, regal bearing, fun-loving, smart appearance, immensely wealthy — interests include jousting, hunting, hawking, eating enormous quantities, dissolving monasteries — seeks sincere lady for short fling or possible long-term relationship. Fairy-tale princesses only — no time-wasters, please. Portrait appreciated. Reply PO Box H8.

SEXUAL CHEMISTRY

GIRL TYPES

Blind Date is all about a little thing called sexual chemistry. Take male element A and mix with female molecule X and see if the test-tube begins to bubble nicely — or will it explode in a blinding flash?

Whatever happens, the whole point is that when picker meets pickee we should get a little more than a damp squib. But how do we make sure we're using the right ingredients? The trick is to select your raw material from the shelves of the great supermarket of romance forearmed with an insight into what **really** makes people tick.

The Barbie Doll

More plastic than a credit card, Miss BD knew from birth that blondes would have more fun. And the annoying thing is, those golden tresses are **real** — the reallest thing about her anyway. But being natural isn't BD's thing, the sort of job she has is all about turning people into what they're not — like being a beauty consultant or an aerobics teacher.
Favourite TV programme — *Dynasty*.

The Girl Next Door

She's natural, open, friendly, a bit of a tomboy, always prepared to laugh at herself and more interested in what concerns other people than in her own ego. She's aware of social issues and would like a job helping people less fortunate than herself. When it comes to romance she's a little bit shy but would **love** a bit of old fashioned wooing.
(Barry Mills writes, 'How come I don't live next door to one of these?')

The Air Hostess

Always smiling, and perfectly groomed, this one always wanted a job where she could meet people — and she got one — tending to the needs of tired executives on RomanceAir. The hostie-type needn't just live her life at 30,000 feet, she's equally at home behind a busy reception desk or personning the phone with that air of quiet confidence — but does she have to be so irritatingly bright and friendly **all** the time?
Favourite actress — Jane Seymour

The girl next door's best friend is her horse

Sunbed Sally

Gold is important to this one, gold chains (lots of them), a golden tan and a gold Amex card for her boyfriend (an older gentleman — genus *Homo Medallionis*). And that tan is glowing all year round — courtesy of two weeks on the Costa Romantica topped up by a weekly session under a few megawatts of ultraviolet. Favourite drink — Kir Royale

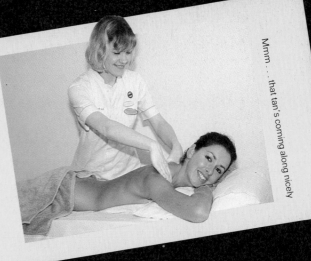

Mmm . . . that tan's coming along nicely

The country girl knows how to muck in . . .

The Country girl

She's **so** nice, the country girl — she'd rather be mucking out her pony than mucking about with boys, but then one has to find a husband and Terry from the village garage may be hunky but he's so unsuitable really. No, the country girl must head for the big city in search of a striped shirted swain. And if Guy or Toby won't take her to the ball, there's always some action on the slopes to look forward to as a chalet maid with all the gang at Obergurgl.
Favourite colour — Welly green

Mrs Zany always knows how to attract attention

Mrs Zany

She likes colossal earrings, and she knows a million things to do with hair gel. She's most at home in a pair of dungarees or outsize culottes — as long as they are acid green or shocking fuschia. Her body is a means of **expression,** of a wild anarchic character that no one can tame — and certainly not Mr Zany.
Favourite actress — Su Pollard

The Hunk

Hey – I really am good looking, aren't I, girls? Nice leather jacket, pair of Levi 501s . . . you know, the ones like that bloke takes off in the launderette. Even got the two-day stubble. Do you think I look like him? I think I do . . .

Favourite star – Myself

The Wimp

He's so nice really . . . but he just won't get on with it. He's given every opportunity – 'come back to my place', 'how about a little goodbye kiss' – the lot, but he just won't go for the clinch. No, romance is not for the wimp. He'd rather be train spotting, or spending a weekend for two walking the Pennine Way.

Favourite item of clothing – Dayglo Cagoule

The Medallion Man

There he is, up against the bar toying with a cocktail. And there **it** is, nestling in a forest of luxuriant chest fur, a glint of gold – a glittering talisman of masculine promise set against a background of tanned, rippling muscle – girt by an arrogant V of slashed white shirt. What a heartbreaker! What macho mystery! . . . What a poser!

Favourite drink – Piña Colada

Beneath his anorak, does the wimp have a romantic heart?

Ray-Ban Man

What's he trying to hide? Even Bruce Willis with a hangover takes his shades off sometimes. No, Ray-Ban man stays shrouded in mystery – day and night. Like James Dean, he's so full of rebellious emotion, he can only communicate in grunts. And he wears those expensive shades because he's sensitive to all those flashing lights in the disco, you see, and anyway he doesn't want any passing paparazzi to know that it's **him**, going out with someone unimportant like you. He's so c-o-o-o-o-o-l it makes you sick.

Favourite colour – black

Ray-Ban man role model James Dean makes hearts go pit-a-pat with or without his shades

The Wolf

Brylcreem never went out of fashion for this guy. He was probably born with slicked back hair and that dreaful Clark Gable moustache. Why does he think he's so sexy? Quasimodo had more pulling power – perhaps that's why he has to work so hard.

He'll promise you champagne and a quick trip down the autoroute to Paris in his Maserati biturbo – but parked outside, you can guarantee, he's got the Maestro loaded with computer stationery samples.

The Regular Guy

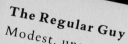

Modest, unassuming, sensitive, loyal, good-looking, kind, generous, courteous, non-smoker, moderate drinker, concerned about the environment, likes animals, likes children . . . dull.

Hero – Prince Charles

Mr Zany

Know the type? Always one for jolly japes and for whom every day is April the 1st. There's a chuckle in every chat-up line and there's nothing better than a party to be the life and soul of – preferably armed with a can of crazy foam.

He's the one in the holiday snap of all the gang relaxing on paella night on the Costa Romantica – wearing the giant-size sunglasses while balancing a bottle of San Miguel on his head.

His wardrobe looks like something Dame Edna would choose for a trip to Honolulu. His idea of snappy dressing is a pair of outrageous Hawaii-pattern shorts and a T-shirt with a **funny** slogan.

Ambition – to be a presenter on children's telly

Don't laugh at me 'cos I'm a clown – Mr Zany can't resist any opportunity for a gag

WHERE TO MEET

So now we know. There are loads of romantics out there all yearning to love and be loved. So how do they get together? OK, we know the Blind Date studio must be the coolest place for that first encounter, but although many are called, few are chosen. But don't despair — if you can't get on the show, you can get it on anywhere else you choose. Let's start with an old favourite — at a **party** . . .

#1 IT'S MY PARTY AND I'LL CRY IF I WANT TO

Why does anyone throw parties? They're expensive, they're messy. The neighbours refuse to talk to you for weeks. There's always a huge red wine stain on your new carpet, a couple you never invited doing very strange things in the **coat room** — and that crashing bore who gate-crashes and then crashes out on the sofa, the one who sneaks off in the morning without helping to clear up the half gnawed chicken legs garnished with fag-ends.

Romantics disregard all this. They love giving parties and going to parties because parties are where romantic things are bound to happen.

For true romantics, the best bit about going to a party happens before you get there. It's the anticipation, the bath, the hairwash, the ritual anointing with perfume or after shave, and the new outfit you bought specially that Saturday afternoon, all so you can stand in some dreadful kitchen, awash with cans of lager and have peanuts spilled all down your front.

ETIQUETTE FOR ROMANTICS
To Kiss or Not to Kiss?
'It is not polite to offer to kiss or be kissed on the first meeting. A brisk good-night with a very grateful thank-you should be given straightaway.'
Mills and Boon's Manners for Moderns 1964

ETIQUETTE FOR ROMANTICS
Tips for Men
'When being introduced to a lady, you should always be standing, your hands should not be in your pockets, you should look interested, should not have a cigarette in your mouth, and — if shaking hands, should not be wearing your gloves . . .'
From *Debrett's Correct Etiquette* 1968

ETIQUETTE FOR ROMANTICS
That First Date — Tips for Young Ladies
'Never stand a boy up. If you have a date with him which you afterwards regret, telephone beforehand with a polite excuse — but if you have to go through with it — do so with good grace.'
From *Debrett's Correct Etiquette* 1968

Cilla Says
I love a good party. I really do. It's been ages since I danced round my handbag!

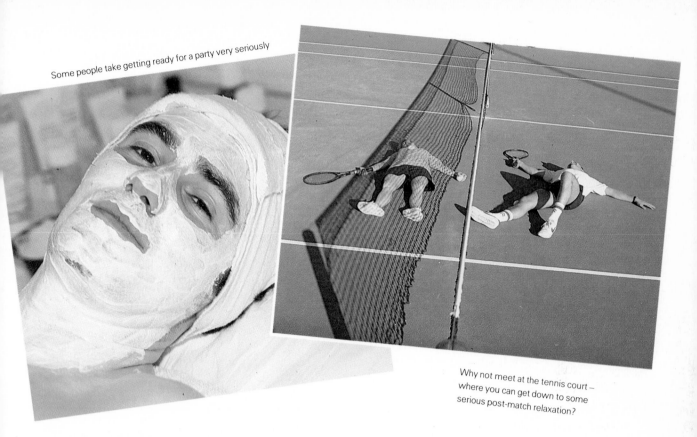

Some people take getting ready for a party very seriously

Why not meet at the tennis court — where you can get down to some serious post-match relaxation?

But romantics don't mind. They're not the type to be standing in the kitchen for long anyway because after anticipation comes the thrill of the chase . . .

#2 THE DISCO

Make it Saturday Night Fever every night of the week by looking for romance down the disco. With that pounding rhythm and those dazzling lights, love might be only a heartbeat away.

#3 THE WINE BAR

It may be yuppie-city but there's more chance of a romantic tête-a-tête over a nice bottle of Bulgarian Chardonnay and some deep-fried Camembert chunks in a candle-lit wine-bar than there is down the boozer on a Chas 'n' Dave knees-up night.

Terrible chat-up line for him 'Hi baby, fancy some house white — round at my house?'

#4 THE FITNESS CENTRE

A good place for romantics to display their perfect rippling bods but who are the guys trying to impress — the girls or each other? All that grunting and groaning sounds like a Chimps' Tea Party.

Terrible chat-up line for her 'Oooh, with a body like that, I'm sure we could work something out . . . '

#5 BY THE BANK CASH MACHINE

Why not liven up those tedious moments waiting for the old dosh-dispenser to cough up the readies by looking for romance in the queue? You never know — it might be the bank which likes to say . . . Yes!

Terrible chat-up line for her 'Take me out tonight and I might show you some additional services before your money is dispensed . . . '

As all Blind Date fans know, an important moment of the show comes when a lucky couple must pick an exotic destination in which to spend their day of days. It could be long haul to Hong Kong or by luxury limo to Lowestoft. But whatever the location, romance is always on the itinerary, because when you are looking for love, it's being a long way from home that makes the heart grow fonder.

So if you still haven't met your perfect partner at a party or had a dalliance down the local launderette — try these suggestions for alien encounters of the romantic kind –

The Costa Romantica

Who cares if the hotel you booked isn't even built yet — or the plumbing looks as if it should never have left the DIY-centre — because on the Costa Romantica, passion is always just around the corner.

Get in the mood with a day on the beach, as firm young bodies turn golden brown under an azure Mediterranean sky. Then why not disco the night away to the romantic rhythms of Agadoo and the Birdy Song?

Next day you can show what you can do on the pedalloes — or why not try a little windsurfing? And the gang's all there for

all the fun of paella night! Sun, sea, sangria and . . . there's something for everyone on the fabulous Costa Romantica.
Guaranteed no surcharges!
— or if you're feeling a little bit more adventurous you could always try . . .

Romance on the Piste

What could be more romantic than a chair-lift built for two, whisking you up the side of some majestic Alpine peak, the air like wine, the snow crisp and firm — with nowhere for you both to go but down.

And girls! Look for romance on the nursery-slopes and the chances are you will find some supertanned Teutonic hunk of a ski-instructor who will show you more than just how to slalom.

Remember, after a hard day pounding the piste — in the evening it's gluhwein-a-gogo round a roaring log fire, with nothing to worry about the morning- après.

Holiday Heartbreak

But beware the holiday romance that fades faster than a sun-tan or melts quicker than the snows of the Val d'Isère in the spring.

You can soothe insect bites and jelly fish stings. You can calm a tummy which is churning away like a cement mixer — but there's no instant cure for the anguish that comes at that moment of reckoning when you must say goodbye to Klaus the handsome ski-instructor from Obergurgl or Maria the raven-haired beauty from Burgos — and Trevor from Preston who promises, promises, that the flames of your passion in the sun will never be put out . . . and, of course, he'll come to Torquay to see you — every weekend.

or you might choose a more unusual spot – like Moscow.
No, you can't bring the entire Red Army choir home with you

ETIQUETTE FOR ROMANTICS

THE RESTAURANT

A romantic dinner for two . . . but watch out! There's a pepper mill concealed in that violin

Why were credit cards invented? For hiring cars? For buying the groceries? Or was it so that chaps could be all posy and executive?

No, those little squares of plastic have one crucial function above anything else. They were designed so that boys could take girls to expensive restaurants.

At the end of that candle-lit dinner for two, our hero can pick up the bill, give a little smirk, flash the plastic and continue his quest for romance – the day of reckoning is weeks away, right now all he's got to worry about is the 'would you like to come back for a coffee?' routine.

Restaurant owners have had this sussed since the first candle was stuck in a Chianti bottle. 'Table for two? Of course, this way . . . I'm sure you would like somewhere quiet.' (Why is it always near the kitchen door?) 'Would sir like to taste the wine? How about this incredibly expensive bottle so you can impress your girlfriend with your exquisite taste and sophistication?' (Ask for house white and that's you rumbled mate.)

Well, it's all nonsense isn't it? Real lovers shouldn't be able to taste a thing. Who cares about looking at the menu when you can look into each other's eyes?

Barry Mills' Romance Report
Which Romantic Restaurant?

#1 Italian
Picture the scene, guys – it's all going great. You've both ordered your favourites and the old Verdicchio is hitting the right spot. Then it happens – the **Italian waiter** comes over, all tight trousers and red shirt waving his bloody great pepper mill.

'Wouldda the lovely senorita likea some black pepper?' he asks.

She goes all gooey – as if Robert de Niro had asked her round to his place. That's it! – she's lost now for the rest of the meal. Every course and out comes the leaning tower of Pisa, grating and grinding away like a demented vacuum cleaner.

#2 Chinese
No problems with pepper mills but how to make romantic small talk while reading a menu full of fish-lips and pig's bowels?

There's always a chance to show off with your chop sticks, but beware! Be sure you really know how to manipulate the old noodle-tongs before you run the risk of dropping a piece of squid in black bean sauce down the front of your trousers.

#3 French
Here's a tip, lads – stay off the garlic if you are going to stay the course. Chewing a crafty Polo doesn't make it. You'll just end up tasting like an After Eight *à la Provencale*.

Candlelit dinners — The Truth!

The eyes, they say, are the windows of the soul. This means that big black pupils are an automatic giveaway. When your pupils dilate it is a sign that you are interested in something or someone. For instance, perhaps you have just seen your ideal blind date across a crowded room.

And your pupils contract when you see something that repels or disgusts you — there's nothing you can do about it.

Or is there?

Dilated pupils are a sign that your partner is interested in you — and pupils automatically dilate when the lights go dim — so when you stare across a romantic candlelit table at your beloved — and yes, he or she is looking back all dark eyed and excited — could it be infatuation?

Or could it be a desperate attempt to read the menu?

How about this one? 'While in a restaurant my dentures fall into the soup. I don't notice because my toupée has slipped over my eyes. What would you do, and do you still want to be picked?'

But when a picker wants to get through to an unseen pickee there's nothing like the 'I've lost my wallet routine' to see if true love might last beyond the coffee and liqueurs . . .

These two are definitely off to a good start

Where's all the food gone?

Jo, play it straight at the restaurant and omance will always be on the menu

Angela Boon's Romance Report

#1 The Italian restaurant

If that waiter waves that bloody great pepper mill in my face again I'll scream!

#2 The Chinese restaurant

Barry . . . what a poser. You know what he told me? 'Love should be like Chinese food — every meal a feast of delicacies, and in an hour's time you want to do it all over again' . . . hmmm.

#3 The French Restaurant

Right, girls — it's the great garlic question. You can see it, can't you? He wants to order something all French and garlicky, like ratatouille, but he's worried about what happens next. For true romantics there's only one thing for it. Order the most garlicky thing on the menu yourself and don't worry about who's going to take whose breath away.

Not everyone feels it's important to dress for dinner

Ristorante Romantica

Come to Ristorante Romantica, the restaurant where
romance is always on the menu

PILAU TALK

From the exotic Orient — hot dishes to inflame hot
passions

Seafood Biryani

Because in love, as in cooking, even the most exotic
combinations of ingredients sometimes need
spicing up

Pappadum

Because love can be brittle — but it's worth picking
up the pieces

Chicken vindaloo and six pints of lager

(not recommended for first dates)

PITTA PATTER

From the balmy shores of the Aegean we present our
romantic Stavros Specials —

Deep fried squid

Because in the game of love, you should never give a
sucker an even break

Greek yoghurt

Because even old goats shouldn't always be ignored

Stuffed vine leaves

Because lovers who may look green on the outside
can have nice things hidden inside

PLAT D' AMOUR

From Paris, city of romance, our chef brings you this
selection of amour-arousers —

Boeuf Bourguinonne

For lovers who find the going tough to begin with
but, soaked in wine for a few hours, they might find
themselves getting all tender

Paté Maison

Because sometimes love can be like a mincing
machine — but it's worth waiting for what comes out
at the end

Coq au Vin

(not recommended for first dates)

Vat inclusive. Service Not Included.

THE FOOD OF LOVE

If you thought it was music, think again. No, when it comes to finding the way to anyone's heart, the shortest route is via the stomach.

...e can be a bowl of strawberries ...en romance is in bloom

Mmmmm . . . yummy

**Barry Mills'
Romance Report**
This is a good one — what are my top romantic breakfast cereals?
All-Bran — because I'm a regular boyfriend
Frosties — because I may not be a tiger in the evening but I can be one at breakfast
Porridge — because I'm just a prisoner of love
Muesli — because I'm nuts about you

Go on . . . just a little teeny weeny clawful

Cilla Says
I love a romantic dinner by candlelight. But if a good nosh is the best recipe for romance, how come I'm always on a diet?

GIFTS OF LOVE
PRESENTS FOR ROMANTICS

'I like to recieve presents as I see them as gifts of love. It is our first date — what would you give me and why?' asked Blind Date picker Rebecca.

A dozen red roses, a single orchid, chocs, underwear, pink champagne, perfume, after-shave — considering all the things in the world true romantics could send to each other, the standard shopping list gets a bit samey. But would you really want to receive a set of spanners or a pair of sensible shoes from your beloved?

American wit Dorothy Parker had this to say about gifts of love —

Why is it no one ever sent me yet,
  One perfect limousine do you suppose?
Ah no, it's always just my luck to get,
  One perfect rose.

One Perfect Rose

A French poet once sent his *amour* a stone rather than flowers because he wanted to be remembered forever (sadly she didn't want to remember him forever, what she wanted was a nice bunch of flowers). Perhaps the poet had forgotten that love, like a garden, has to be constantly worked at and renewed to stay in bloom. So perhaps presents that can be guzzled or swilled — like chocolate and champagne — represent the here today gone tomorrow, type of love.

See if you agree — try the The Blind Date Consumer Test on Romantic Presents and try and spot the **real** motive behind all those hearts and flowers . . .

Which Romantic Present?
Why Give What to Whom?

Questions for the Girls

He gives you a big bunch of red roses. What do you think?
a That his passion is overflowing?
b That he must work in a garden centre?
c That he's an unimaginative twerp?

He sends you a single red rose. What do you think?
a That you're the only one for him?
b That he bought a whole bunch and is doling out the rest to 11 other girls?
c That he's a tight-fisted meanie?

You send him a Venus Fly Trap. What are you trying to tell him?
a That you want your heart to be completely captured by him?
b That the only thing he could attract would be an insect?
c That his flies are undone?

He sends you plastic flowers. Why, do you think?
a Because he wants your love to last forever?
b Because a real flower couldn't match your beauty?
c Because he's completely artificial?

He sends you a stone. Is this because —
a He wants to be remembered forever?
b He's a Flintstones fan?
c This relationship is really dead?

A single perfect rose – the ideal gift of love?

Questions for the Chaps

You send her an enormous bunch of red roses. Is it because —

a You **are** overflowing with passion?
b You **do** work in a garden centre?
c You **are** an unimaginative twerp?

You send her a single red rose. Is it because —

a She's the only one for you?
b That you **have** got loads of girlfriends and can only afford a single rose each?
c That you **are** a tight-fisted meanie?

You send her a cactus. Is it because —

a Your love is so rare that it only blooms once every hundred years?
b She's got a spiky personality?
c She'd be at home in a desert?

You've forgotten to buy her anything on her birthday. Do you —

a Take her out and make it up to her?
b Tell her not to be so pathetic — that your love is above such things?
c Hide?

You send her a volume of romantic poetry. Is this because —

a You can't put into words what you feel?
b You think she needs educating?
c You found it cheap in a remainder shop?

No — don't mess around when it comes to romantic presents. Give your beloved something unusual and they'll only end up completely misinterpreting it. Much better to play safe and stick to flowers, chocolates and perfume — but even here you have to be careful — **as we shall see . . .**

HEARTS AND FLOWERS

For a chap to send his beloved a bunch of flowers would seem pretty straightforward. A big bunch of roses, a single orchid, a huge spray of pink carnations — nothing can go wrong, surely?

But did you know there was a language of flowers? You might send her some specially selected bunch which could actually say something very different from the message you had in mind.

The idea that you could send romantic communications with plants is a very ancient one — the Greeks and Romans were at it like crazy and the sultans of the Ottoman Empire liked nothing better than to send floral love letters to the chosen ones of the harem. There was a huge vogue in Victorian England for sending secret messages of love via flowers and these secret messages needed a secret code which the recipient would work out with a pounding heart — like this . . .

You Bring the Thought — We'll Bring the Flowers

If you want to tell your loved one something — this is what to send (but we can't guarantee Interflora could come up with Dogsbane or Judas Tree at short notice).

Angela Boon's Romance Report

Barry's coming to supper so I thought I'd pop down to Sainsbury's for some extra groceries. I bought a quarter of mushrooms, some mustard, some lettuce, some vine leaves, and an apple and bilberry yoghurt. I hope Barry gets the message from that lot — that he's treacherous, drunken, indifferent and cold-hearted — and that I'm deeply suspicious but could still be tempted!

It's the thought that counts

Affection — Dwarf sunflower	**Excess, beware of** — Saffron	**Indifference** — Mustard seed
Am I forgotten? — Holly	**Faithfulness** — Heliotrope	**Insincerity** — Foxglove
Anticipation — Gooseberry	**Falsehood** — Bugloss, Dogsbane	**I want you back** — Jonquil
Bashfulness — Peony	**Fascination** — Carnation	**Keep your promise** — Plum tree
Beautiful eyes — Variegated tulip	**Fickleness** — Pink larkspur	**Love** — Myrtle
Beauty — Red rose	**Fidelity** — Ivy	**Love at first sight** —
Beauty is your only attraction — Japanese rose	**Forget me not** — Forget me not	Arkansa Coreopsis
Betrayal — Judas tree	**Forsaken** — Willow	**Marriage** — Ivy
Bond of love — Monthly honeysuckle	**Gossip** — Cobaea	**Platonic love** — Rose acacia
Cold-hearted — Lettuce	**Grief** — Aloe, Marigold	**Pleasure and pain** — Dog rose
Consumed by love — Syrian mallow	**Happy love** — Bridal rose	**Pretended love** — Catchfly
Cure for heartache — Cranberry	**Heartlessness** — Hydrangea	**Secret love** — Yellow acacia
Dangerous pleasures — Tuberose	**Hopeless love** — Yellow tulip	**Suspicion** — Mushroom
Deceitful charms — Thorn-apple	**I am dazzled by you** — Ranunculus	**Rendezvous** — Chickweed
Devotion — Heliotrope	**I am captivated by you** — Peach blossom	**Sensuality** — Spanish jasmine
Drunkenness — Vine	**I love you** — Red chrysanthemum	**Temptation** — Apple, Quince
Esteem but not love — Spiderwort	**Inconstant love** — Wild honeysuckle	**Treachery** — Bilberry

The wild bunch

Do you think this is ridiculous? Well no more so than kissing under the mistletoe or pulling off the petals of a daisy chanting 'she loves me, she loves me not' . . . And look at how long people have been believing in this leafy language of love.

Myrtle, for example, the bloom of love, was dedicated by the Greeks to Aphrodite and by the Romans to Venus, the goddesses of love. As legend would have it, when Venus was surprised by a bunch of satyrs as she rose from bathing in the sea, she hid behind a myrtle bush.

The Greenhouse Effect
'Plant-psychologist' Pierre Paul Sauvin of New Jersey discovered that plants react strongly to human romantic emotions. He wired his plants to an oscillator and, as he and his girlfriend made love, the needle went off the dial.

CHOC HORROR

What ranks with flowers as a traditional gift of love? Flowers may wither and die but a big box of chocs could keep your loved one chomping away for days, thinking of you with each soft centre.

If the British love anything we love chocolate. We eat 10,000,000,000 Smarties each year and between Christmas and Easter more than 200 million Creme Eggs slither their gooey way down our throats. Perhaps the face you love wouldn't exactly light up if you sent a tube of Smarties, but chocolate has a long history of romantic connotations.

A Short History of Cupid's Compulsive Confection

Like that other compulsion, tobacco, chocolate was first brought back from the New World by Spanish adventurers who were introduced to the royal drink xocoatl made from ground cacao beans at the court of the Aztec ruler Montezuma.

Opinions differed as to whether this somewhat bitter distillation really was the food of the gods. The Pope drank a cup and found it so disgusting that he was sure no one would make a habit of it and there was no need to ban it during Lent.

But chocolate was beginning to acquire a different reputation — did it have aphrodisiac effects? The Peruvian Indians thought that it did. Centuries later the Versailles-cruising mistress of Louis XV Madame du Barry doled out chockies to her bewigged lovers and Casanova declared that he drank cocoa instead of champagne to get in the mood.

There were attempts by the church to ban chocolate because it seemed to 'inflame monks with passion' and nineteenth century moralists viewed chockie-abuse with prurient suspicion.

Well, what's the truth?

Chocolate contains caffeine and theobromine, both of which are stimulants. Psychologists have discovered that people 'in love' do have different things going on in their body. They radiate a kind of rosy glow of health and vitality actually caused by an increase in the production of chemical messengers in the brain, attitude-adjusting hormones such as phenylethylamine which raise the heartbeat, increase arousal, widen the pupils and which can also cause hyperactivity, blushing and general disorientation — all round romantic silliness in fact.

Chocolate-stuffing by those unlucky in love may be an unconscious attempt to keep up the levels of such natural, internal stimulants. So next time you find yourself all alone with a whole box of Black Magic, and feel tempted to munch your way through the lot, it could be love you're looking for, not soft centres.

Angela Boon's Romance Report

Oh God, Barry's given me a box of Milk Tray. It's not the fact that he knows I'm on a diet I mind — but did he have to burst into my bedroom wearing a ridiculous James Bond outfit and make such a terrible mess all over the floor?

The Language of Chocolate

If flowers can have a language — why not chocolate?
If you can't run to an ultra-expensive glittering box full
of exquisite hand-made truffles, don't worry —
because all you need do is nip down to the corner shop
armed with the

Blind Date Guide to the meaning of chockie bars —

What it means when you give your beloved a bar of —

Marathon — I want to go the distance with you

Rolo — You look all smooth on the outside — but
you've a big soft gooey centre

Milky Bar — You're a stupid looking twit with big specs

Aero — You've got a bubbly personality

After Eight — I'd like to stay till after eight, nine, ten . . .

M+Ms — I look at you and go mmmmmmmm . . .

Lion Bar — You're a great big pussy cat

Yorkie — Love is never having to say you're a lorry

For you my darling

Bounty — You're a taste of Paradise

Mars — You're out of this world

Crunchie — Bees make honey — and you know about
the birds and the bees

And all because the lady loves . . . a nice box of chockies

A WHIFF OF SEDUCTION

HEAVENLY SCENTS FOR REAL ROMANTICS

But if you decide after all that, that chocolate isn't the perfect gift of love, or you can't get quite your message over with a bar of Double-Decker — there is something else you can give your beloved without fear of giving offence. You guessed it — something smelly . . .

You just splash it on all over. . .

What They Ask — About Perfume

If you could have a perfume named after you what would it be called and why?

Number 1

I have got a perfume named after me — it's called 'Mantrap'

Number 2

I'd call it 'Little Red Riding Hood' because when I'm wearing it all the wolves whistle

Number 3

My perfume would have to be called 'Mysterious' because like all good mysteries I need further investigation

BLANDATE
The aftershave for REAL men — with new instant stubble!

For a really masculine tang just splash a bit of Blandate on where it matters. Its secret ingredients will give you that 'I haven't shaved for two days' look — **in seconds.**

Choose from these stubble-settings —

*Splash on once for Mickey Rourke
*Splash on twice for George Michael
*Leave on overnight for that Bob Geldof look

Blind Date
Parfum de LWT

When a man you've never met before walks up and starts asking you some very interesting personal questions — you know that it's all because of Blind Date, the fabulous perfume created especially for you.
Sensuous, exotic, as subtle as you are —
Ozone-friendly!
Parfum and eau de toilette in handy 1-litre bottles.

WHICH WEEPIE?

BLIND DATE AT THE MOVIES

Now you've got your aftershave or perfume on, and one of you is clutching an enormous box of chocs, it's time for that first date — and what's most people's idea of an ideal thing to do? It's going to the movies together. It couldn't be better — you don't have to say anything . . . you don't even have to look at each other. You just sit in the dark for two hours with as many pop-corn and Kia-Ora cartons as you can carry and watch a story about other people.

But that's just the beginning — as the story unfolds — full, we hope, of passion, intensity and excitement — one of you can discreetly reach over and give the other's hand a little squeeze.

Simple as that. You may be surrounded by dozens of other people but there's no embarrassment. Couples have been going for that first little squeeze in the dark since the movies began. In fact, you can bet a good proportion of the paying customers in your average cinema audience are more concerned about when to go for the squeeze than they are about whether ET is going to get home.

So, what sort of film to see on that first date? Sensitive romantics have the answer to this one — a **foreign** film, with subtitles of course. Something French or Swedish is ideal, preferably full of symbolism and **deep** meanings which you can talk about afterwards. He might secretly rather go and see *Freddy's Revenge Seven* but on a first date all true romantics love the sloppy bits.

Sloppy Bits

In fact some of the best films in movie history are those with the most sloppy bits — you know, the ones about doomed love affairs, where the stars spend ages staring into each other's eyes and declaring how their forbidden love can never be.

You know the formula —
Boy meets girl — he is
a incredibly rich
b unhappily married
c dying of an incurable disease

— she is
a incredibly poor
b unhappily married
c dying of an incurable disease

> **MORE ETIQUETTE FOR ROMANTICS**
> **At the Cinema**
> 'With a shy type of girl it is better for the boy to say "let's have some sweets", rather than "would you like some sweets?" as she may otherwise be compelled to refuse.'
> *Mills and Boon's Manners for Moderns*
> 1964

There can be all sorts of permutations but the important thing is that everything's incredibly difficult, but love conquers all until we get to either a huge blubby sad ending or a huge weepy happy ending.

It may be terrible schlock but there's nothing like a good old-fashioned tearjerker to guarantee a squeeze in the dark. Blind Date presents its star-studded selection of all-time Weepie Greats . . .

For Twentysomethings
AN OFFICER AND A GENTLEMAN

Richard Gere is determined to make it through the supertough training course to become a US Navy jet pilot. There's a horrible drill instructor who shouts at him all the time, but he finds comfort with Debra Winger, a girl from a local factory. There's lots of class friction of the 'our love cannot be' kind but after all that — 'love takes them up where they belong'.

Romance Rating ★

ENDLESS LOVE

Brooke Shields plays Jade, the 15-year-old daughter of suburban parents. Jade takes it for granted that David, her intense college-boy beau can stay the night. But Dad says no — so David goes potty and burns down the house! He gets sent away for psychiatric treatment — but years later he is still looking for Jade and guess what — young love has survived even all this!

Romance Rating ★

For Thirtysomethings
THE GRADUATE

He (Dustin Hoffman) is a young, rich Californian suburbanite named Ben. He is seduced by an older woman (Ann Bancroft) but falls in love with her daughter Elaine (Katharine Ross, later to surface bizarrely as Jeff Colby's mother in *Dynasty*-clone, *The Colbys*). Mum goes barmy and tries to wreck their love affair. Meanwhile her daughter becomes reluctantly engaged to someone else. On the brink of Elaine saying 'I do' to Mr Wrong, Ben bursts into the chapel and carries her off. Happy ending.

Romance Rating ★★

A MAN AND A WOMAN (*Un Homme et une Femme*)

This is a film with sub-titles, so it's automatically romantic — but the main characters don't have much to say anyway.

This French film, made in the mid 1960s, actually invented all the clichés used for romance imagery in films and adverts ever since — couples running along beaches in slow motion, kissing in the rain, lots of camera blurs, tint and soft focus and, when the plot begins to pall, cutting to gambolling horses, lambs — even dogs.

The plot is simple, **she** (Anouk Aimée) is a script girl who falls for racing driver Jean Louis Trintignant. Both have lost their first spouses so there's a lot of moping about before they get down to business.

Romance Rating ★★

LOVE STORY

He (Ryan O'Neal) is a preppy brat from a stuffy, old-money family. **She** (Ali MacGraw) is a beautiful fellow-student — but she comes from the wrong side of town. They fall in love against the odds — it's all great but guess what — she's dying from an incurable disease. She dies — it's all terribly sad.

'Love is never having to say you're sorry' was the film's most famous line — but what does it mean?

Romance Rating ★★★★

For Fortysomethings
BRIEF ENCOUNTER

You remember this one. **She** (Celia Johnson who talks just like the Queen) is married to boring, pipe-smoking Freddy. She meets **him,** a local doctor, by chance in a station buffet when **he** (Trevor

Howard) takes a speck of soot out of her eye. From here on in it's forbidden love among the stale buns with passionate Rachmaninov music welling up at the drop of Trevor's trilby. But their love cannot be, he disappears forever on the 9.25 to Effingham Junction and she goes back to Freddy and his stamp collection.
Romance Rating ★★★★

WATERLOO BRIDGE

Fifty years old yet still an all-time tearjerker. Duke's nephew (Robert Taylor) marries ballerina (Vivien Leigh) against his snooty family's wishes. He is reported missing in the war and she sinks into penury and prostitution. But he's not dead and years later they meet again — Blub!
Romance Rating ★★★

NOW VOYAGER

Tear-stained variation of the Cinderella story. A psychiatrist (played by Claude Rains) gives sexually repressed, dowdy Bette Davis the confidence to look for love. **She** finds it with Paul Henreid — but their affair is doomed. Contains perhaps the most famous scene in weepie film history — Henreid lighting two cigarettes and tenderly handing one to Davis — and her parting line to him 'Don't ask for the moon — we have the stars' . . .
Romance Rating ★★★★

Cilla Says

I love a film with lots of sloppy bits. Just stock up on the tissues, buy a big box of chox and have a good old cry — some say it's less trouble than the real thing!

Barry Mills' Romance Report

I suppose I'd better take Angela to the cinema. But what would she like? . . . some old weepy film I guess — full of sloppy bits. There's that new Dirty Harry film and Clint would make my day . . . but she wants romance, not sex and violence . . .

Angela Boon's Romance Report

Barry rang . . . and suggested we go to the movies. He wants to take me to some terrible old Hollywood tearjerker . . . Oh Gawd! Now there's that new Clint Eastwood I wouldn't mind seeing.

Forbidden Romance

Their Blind Date ended in more than tears!

Get your hankies ready – this makes other weepies look like Postman Pat!

TRUE ROMANCE

TRY A LITTLE FANTASY

If you find the course of true love doesn't always run quite smoothly, if the hurts of real life are getting too much to bear, then there's a whole fantasy world to lose yourself in — and a huge industry out there to help you. Unlike munching your way through a box of chocolates, you will find their products completely safe and non-fattening. When the going gets tough, the romantic go shopping — for a good old-fashioned love story.

The thing about romantic fiction is that it is so dependable.

Romance books **all** have happy endings. There is only one plot — the story of two people who fall in love, and their story will follow a set pattern —

The Blind Date Guide to How to Write a Soppy Love Story

1 Attractive **woman** (she is independent and mature, aged between 23 and 29, intelligent, accomplished, middle class — nowadays she is probably a professional, a doctor or a lawyer perhaps) meets a devastating **man.**

2 He is eight to 12 years older than the heroine, self-assured, masterful, hot-tempered, capable of violence, passion and tenderness . . . often mysteriously moody . . . He is always tall, muscular (but not muscle-bound). He is not necessarily handsome, but is most definitely virile . . . he may be divorced, provided it is made clear in the plot-line that his ex-wife sought the divorce.

They met on Blind Date

— a collision course to happiness!

*One publisher of love stories recommends its authors to get in the mood for romantic outpourings by bathing in scented bath oils and to write wearing silk negligées, surrounded by perfumed candles while listening to seductive, soft background music

* Many authors of romantic fiction are men — who almost invariably write under female pseudonyms

3 They are compulsively attracted to each other — but there are forbidding obstacles to their love. There are **big problems** to get over on the path to true romance. One of them could be the other woman who is depicted as ambitious, possessive and generally nasty.

4 They are torn apart.

5 Steps **3** and **4** can be repeated for additional intrigue.

6 They triumph over the obstacles which a cruel world has set in their path. At last they are in each other's arms and on course for marriage and a happy ending.

Simple as that. Set this plot in a hospital, in a solicitor's office, in Regency England, on a tropical island, in a crumbling Gothic house . . . in a space ship.

Sex is not a problem. Lack of it is what keeps the excitement going until the final dénouement, but there are lots of nods and winks on the way.

Sex can be 'sweet' (kissing and cuddling), 'spicy' (sensuous touching above the waist) or 'steamy' (buy one and find out). But anything steamy must be reserved for the final chapter and before we get there, tension builds with furtive glances, electrically charged kisses, pounding hearts, shivering flares of emotion — pain, anger, ecstasy, jealousy, grief, frustration.

Or you can have the real thing

ROMANCE ON WHEELS

'They say people's cars reflect their personalities. What kind of car do you imagine I drive?' is the sort of question Blind Date pickers ask.

John knows something that all true romantics know, that love without a set of wheels is like a breakfast TV presenter without a cuddly pullover.

Well, what sort of car would you like to think people associated **you** with? A Ferrari Testa Rossa? . . . or a Porsche 944 perhaps? How about a shell-pink vintage Hispano-Suiza? Or does it come down to a Skoda Estelle or a Reliant Robin? You see, motor cars have nothing to do with getting from A to B. When it comes to romance, you are what you drive.

As far as those who sell cars are concerned, road-going romantics are never stuck in an eight-mile tailback on the M25. They never have to slog down to Tesco's on a rainy Friday night for a boot-load of groceries, only to find the supermarket car park is full when they get there. And you can forget all the technical stuff. Who cares about what's going on under the bonnet when true romantics have a whole different kind of pulling power to worry about.

No, in car fantasy-world, chaps are always driving along completely empty roads through majestic, craggy scenery — or careering through Australian cane fields which mysteriously burst into flames as they pass. Must be something to do with the exhaust.

The girls are just as bad. They're always in hot little hatchbacks, usually flaming red, a colour chosen to match the colour of their lipstick, cutting up the yuppie sales manager in the company car park.

The trouble is that all this TV and advertising imagery actually works. If first impressions are what matter, it's no good turning up on that Blind Date in a rusting Cortina full of fuzzy dice and nodding dogs. If you happen to be reading this in a car well, you should be keeping your eyes on the road, but next time you are stopped at the lights, take a look around you. See that bloke over there? The one driving a black go-fast Teutonic number. He's probably using his carphone to tell his mum he's going to be late home. And what about her over there in the yellow Suzuki four-wheel-drive fun-jeep, all streaked blond mane and dark glasses? She probably needs all that off-road performance just to get her hair-do home.

Angela Boon's Car Report

'I'm Sorry, I Seem To have Run Out of Petrol'

It's great, isn't it? He's trying to be all cool and sophisticated. He's taken you out in his swanky car full of knobs and switches with the gear-lever in one of those little leather bags — regaling you with stories about how he's really got it all under control. If he's so fantastic, how come he forgot a little thing like putting some petrol in the tank before we set out? So what do you do?

He suggests we cuddle up together under this convenient blanket he has in the back.

I suggest he gets out and starts walking to the nearest garage.

Daters get up to all sorts of things on the
re, and who needs a fast set of wheels
en you're in love?

Limo-love is fun, but this
could be stretching a point

No . . . no, the car's meant to be four wheel drive, not
you

That's why I fell for the leader of the pack

Whatever cars may say about us as
individuals, there's no doubt about it,
piling into a spankers new motor and
heading off to some exotic destination is a
sure way of getting your romance on the
road. It may not always be a case of
cruising effortlessly along open roads in
some fabulous ragtop sports car, hair
blowing in the breeze — it may be more
like bumper to bumper on the A34 in a
rusting Ford Capri — hardly Miami Vice,
is it?

Whether Clacton or Cannes is your
destination, a car is the only romantic way
to travel — and do you know why?
Because cars can sometimes **run out of
petrol . . .**

Something flash does have a certain pulling
power

Romancing The Bean

Romantic Etiquette for Coffee-Lovers

Forget champagne, forget piña colada – what is the magic potion that really fuels the fires of romance?

You know the scene. **He** knocks on **her** door. There's no scraping bolts, no shuffling of carpet slippers from within. This is the stuff that gets instant action.

The door opens. There's a hint of rag rolling and Laura Ashley flounces in a softly lit room.

She is standing there, radiant, beautiful, a hint of older-woman mystery around the eyes. He is tall, his body lean and firm, a ready smile plays round his well cut jawline. He holds a mysterious empty container in his hand.

Their eyes meet, their pupils dilate . . . you can feel their heartbeats quickening. He speaks . . .

'I seem to have run out of teabags.'

No . . . it just doesn't work somehow. The mysterious tropical bean — Kenya, Java, Brazilian, Colombian, Blue Mountain, black, white, filter, espresso, cappaccino, bean, ground or instant, whatever your fancy — **coffee** is the key to the door of romance.

Just think how many romances have stumbled at that vital point where the crucial question is asked . . . 'would you like to come inside for a *coffee?*' . . .

Barry Mills' Romance Report

Well, I tried it.
Went upstairs and knocked on the door of Number 4 clutching empty jar of Blend 88.

Voice from within says, 'Who is it?'

'Hello,' I say. 'I'm Barry from downstairs – I seem to have run out of coffee.'

Door opened by six foot tall bloke holding a welding torch.

'Why don't you try Tesco's, mate?'

Ah well . . .

Angela Boon's Romance Report

Went to this really posh dinner party last night.
It was all candlelight and curly lettuce.
This guy turns up at the door clutching a jar of something.
Our hostess turns to him and says –
'Ugh – Instant! I can't give my guests that!'

Cilla Says

I'll shake the coffee beans — oh, but if only they could be percolated!

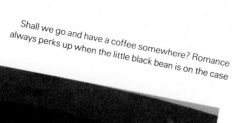

Shall we go and have a coffee somewhere? Romance always perks up when the little black bean is on the case

While some Blind Daters prefer the more direct approach when they're down the caff . . .

Would You Like to Come Inside for a Coffee?

It's a real giveaway, isn't it? It doesn't matter who is making the running, girl or boy, those magic words have a place in romantic etiquette as important as 'Are you dancing?'.

'Come inside for a cup of cocoa' just doesn't make it and nobody's interested in etchings any more. No, going through the coffee barrier is the hurdle serious romantics have to leap . . . and chaps! Just think how clever you will seem when you entertain your pickee with your vocal impersonation of a coffee percolator!

The Morning After

If you're not worn out by all that coming inside for a coffee, making stupid plot-plot noises, playing backgammon and keeping Italian waiters awake the night before, real romantic coffee lovers can start all over again as soon as dawn breaks. Because the seductive bean is on the job 24 hours a day.

That must be the big problem for coffee advertisers. Do they go for the night before with all those candlelit suppers and bottomless coffee-pots – or do they go for the morning after when everyone's leaping around grinning manically, looking super-fit on six hours sleep, and producing handfuls of coffee beans like demented conjurers to shake at each other?

GOING FOR THE CLINCH

ETIQUETTE FOR ROMANTICS
Advice to Single Girls

#1

'Think three times before you go to a man's flat if he is, or will be, alone — again it is a question of avoiding misunderstanding.'

#2

'It is never wise to go out with a married man — except under the most open conditions — and even then, one invitation is about all you should accept.'

From the *Vogue Book of Etiquette* (1969)

A nifty bit of life-saving is always a good opener

After all that wooing there comes a point for all romantics when they must actually go for it! . . . It's never too late for a cuddle

What if you've tried everything, the romantic restaurant, the weepie film, the smoochy party? What if you have showered the object of your affection with chocs, flowers, perfume and poetry — and still nothing has happened? For those with big bank balances we offer these suggestions —

* Hire a plane with a banner behind it saying 'I Love You' — cost £450
* Hire an advertising hoarding — a mere £350 for a month
* Hire a famous actor/actress to go and read some sloppy poem along with your message of love — cost £500+
* Take a full page colour advertisement in a national newspaper — a bargain at £35,000

Classier than carving BARRY LOVES ANGELA TRUE on a tree we think you'll agree — but a mite expensive. No, if your loved one hasn't got the message by now, this relationship might be turning into the biggest non-event since . . . ?

What one of you has got to do is **go for the clinch.** These days it doesn't really matter who takes the first step, him or her — as long as you both know that exquisite moment is going to come when you can look into each other's eyes and say 'I love you'.

So why hang about with all that 'well maybe', 'perhaps', 'I think you're really nice . . . but'.

Go on! Won't one of you please give the other one a big smacker!

Now I've got you where I want you . . .

These Blind Daters haven't quite got the hang of the clinch

Blackpool PLEASURE BEACH

'I JUST CALLED TO SAY I LOVE YOU'

TELEPHONE TORMENT

There's something that romantics, despite the fact that they love it and hate it all at the same time, cannot do without. It's the telephone. Hearts still pound and palms still go sweaty at the tremulous chirrup of Cupid's cocoa-tin.

This is how it goes. Boy meets girl at a party. The big moment arrives — will she give him her **telephone number**? She does — and he makes that most romantic of gestures — writing her telephone number on his **hand**. Now we get to the difficult bit.

The Next Day
10.00am WHAT HE'S THINKING
It's the morning after the night before. Her phone number is lovingly inscribed in ball point on his hand. He likes her a lot but he's worried. He's got to be cool. How did he leave it last night? 'Ciao, baby — I'll bell you' — well, that was pretty cool. He knows what to do — he'll let her wait a bit . . . and then he'll ring her.

10.00 am WHAT SHE'S THINKING
She's at home with mum. She met this really nice boy last night and gave him her phone number. She really liked him, but she doesn't want him to think that she doles out her number to everyone she meets. Still, it would be nice if he did ring — but what can she do? She has an idea. 'Look, Mum, if this bloke rings — tell him I'm out.' Yes, that should do it.

12.00 am WHAT HE'S THINKING
'Perhaps she gave her number to that other bloke she was with in the kitchen . . . no . . . no, she seemed to like me, she really did. I'll let it go another hour.'

12.00 am WHAT SHE'S THINKING
'Anybody rung for me, Mum? Nobody?'

2.00 pm WHAT HE'S THINKING
'I'm sure it was that bloke in the kitchen. Oh God, what if I ring and she's with him?'

2.00 pm WHAT SHE'S THINKING
'Perhaps he had loads of numbers written on his hand — I bet he's with that tarty looking girl on the stairs.'

3.00 pm WHAT HE'S THINKING
'OK, this is it. I'm going to ring and be all cool and casual. Oh no! It's rubbed off!'

3.00 pm WHAT SHE'S THINKING
'Right, he's with that girl. If he doesn't ring in the next 10 minutes — that's it!'

3.05 pm WHAT HE'S THINKING
'Yes, I can just make it out — right, I'm going to ring her . . . be cool.'

3.05 pm WHAT SHE'S THINKING
'Mum — if this bloke rings, I'm out all day, in fact I'm out forever.'

Remember, the telephone is a treacherous instrument — you never know **who** might be listening in. Just imagine if Romeo and Juliet had had to communicate by phone.

Romeo & Juliet

A Tragedy

Dramatis personae
Romeo Montague
Juliet Capulet
Signor Capulet, Juliet's father, sworn enemy of the Montagues
Man in doublet
Telephone operator

Scene I —*The Capulets' garden in old Verona. Above is a window balcony where Juliet stands bathed in moonlight. She carries a cordless telephone.*

Juliet Romeo, Romeo. Wherefore art thou, Romeo?

Scene II — *A telephone box in the Piazza Romantica. Romeo enters.*

Romeo Damn! It's a cardphone. Wait a minute — I'll try reversing the charges. *(he dials)*
Romeo Operator? Look I'm in a telephone box . . . yes, it's a cardphone and I've only got ducats — yes, yes . . . I want to make a reverse charge call to Verona 34673 . . . a Ms J. Capulet, got that? Yes . . . My name? It's Mr Romeo Montague, yes, R-O-M-E-O — but if her father answers, it's not me, tell him I'm selling double glazing or something, tell him anything but not my name . . . yes . . . I'll wait, thank you . . .
Man in doublet outside telephone box 'Scuse me mate, you going to be all day?
Juliet's voice Hello.
Operator's voice Hello, Ms J. Capulet? I have a transfer charge caller for you — Mr R. Montague. Will you accept the call?
Juliet's voice (excitedly) Oh yes, yes, I'll accept it . . . put him on.
Romeo (sexily) Ciao bambina . . . it's me!
The voice of Juliet's father (gruffly) Hello, hello . . . who's that?
Romeo Oh my God, it's her father! He's picked up the phone downstairs! Er . . . hello, Mr Capulet, er . . . er . . . you have been selected by the Renaissance Double Glazing Company to have your . . . er Campanile reglazed entirely free of charge . . . er. . .
Phone goes dead . . . bzzzzzzzzzzzzz

Scene III — *The Balcony*

Juliet (sighs) Oh Romeo, Romeo. **Wherefore** art thou Romeo!?!

Will he, won't he?

LOVE HURTS

JEALOUSY

Blind Daters are a jealous lot. When a picker wants to probe the personalities of those potential partners lurking behind the screen, there's nothing better than a **loaded question** to get to the truth — and a question about jealousy does very nicely.

Take her out to a restaurant and is she going to flirt with everything in trousers? Take him out for a cosy dinner *à deux* and is he going to wimp on and on about his former girlfriend? Or — if this Blind Date turns into a meaningful relationship — is your partner going to stifle you completely with possessiveness, constantly making you prove your love?

Jealousy can be a relationship-wrecker but it can also be a very positive emotion. It's the flip side of true love, a statement that you really are potty about your partner, potty enough to feel more than a little hot and bothered about somebody else muscling in on your territory.

'You were ogling that waiter all evening' 'No, I wasn't.' 'Yes, you were!'

An extensive survey on jealousy conducted in 1983 discovered that you are more likely to be jealous if —

— You are insecure
— You are living with but not married to your partner
— You have older brothers — the more older brothers you have the more jealous you are likely to be
— For men only — you have a low opinion of yourself to start with

You are less likely to be jealous if —

— You yourself are faithful
— You have sisters or younger brothers
— You are satisfied with your partner

And jealousy can be used creatively to spice up a romance that is — how shall we say — in need of a little refreshment. You know the signs — he says someone else's name in his sleep. She pulls out a box of matches from a restaurant he certainly never took her to. Are they really giving away a deadly secret — or are they using the oldest trick in the book to bring a lover back into line? Just a hint, mind, that there might, perhaps, just possibly that there could be — **someone else.**

If you feel a little bit of jealousy could do the trick, Blind Date offers you another unique service . . .

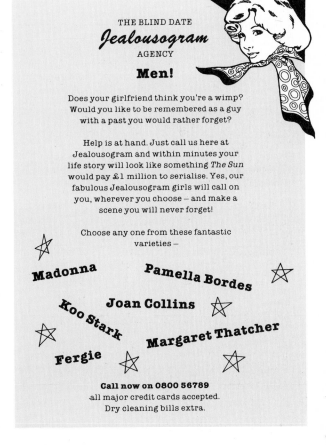

COMMUNICATION BREAKDOWN

Love Hurts —

But the course of true love doesn't always run true. How can anyone expect it to? When you join two people together, 'love' must be the worst excuse in the world for doing so — lovers, after all, are expected to behave as if they have temporarily gone insane, what with all that reverting to babyhood and everything. And as will be obvious to those of us who have been around a bit, not to say **stung** on the nettle-girt pathway of romance, pooky pips and my little sausage will soon be having a good old ding-dong.

The psychologists say that arguments are a vital part of a healthy relationship. But why do they happen?

The Most Common Cause of Arguments Between Couples

1 Money	does what
2 Each other's	**5** Sex
3 Children (whether to	**6** Each other's friends
have them and, when	**7** Jealousy
you've got them, families	**8** Excessive drinking
how to bring them up)	**9** Work
4 Housework — who	**10** The bathroom (!?!)

ETIQUETTE FOR ROMANTICS

How to End a Relationship

'Simply fail to make contact with the other person and politely decline any invitations.'

From the *Vogue Book of Etiquette* (1969)

How to Say NO

'Just going home has a lot in its favour — but this won't be popular with an eager person out for a night's pleasure.'

Claire Rayner's *Safe Sex Pocketbook* (1987)

How to end a relationship the Blind Date way

ETIQUETTE FOR ROMANTICS

Dos and Don'ts of Arguments

'The amount of energy and emotion generated by a thoroughgoing argument can be very exciting . . . you get up a great head of steam and then release it in a burst of love-making.'

From *Claire Rayner's Marriage Guide* (1984)

Well if you're rowing all the time about the bathroom — then someone's left the cold tap running in your relationship. But don't despair — if you find you're not seeing eye to eye most of the time, follow our exclusive **BLIND DATE LOVERS' TIFF CHART** to see where your romance is going.

LOVERS' TIFFS —
WHERE IS YOUR ROMANCE HEADING?

START HERE

Do you argue?

YES ☐   NO ☐

Is the subject on which you argue serious — money, family, sex, the bathroom, etc, or completely trivial ie Bros, *Neighbours*, ex-boyfriends, ex-girlfriends, football, car accessories, etc.

Is it because you don't like arguing?

YES ☐   NO ☐

SERIOUS ☐   TRIVIAL ☐

Or because there's nothing to argue about?

YES ☐   NO ☐

Do you find that after an argument you understand more about each other?

Well, it may seem trivial to you but I think it's very important!

Do you like being so cosy?

YES ☐   NO ☐

YES ☐   NO ☐

Well, you're pretty pleased with yourself, aren't you?

Do you think there are **deep** problems which make you keep arguing?

YES ☐   NO ☐

Would you like to hurl the closest thing that comes to hand at your partner?

YES ☐   NO ☐

Well, keep at it — you're pretty well like any other couple in love

SAD END
This relationship isn't going anywhere.

OK, OK, so nobody's perfect – not even me!

HAPPY ENDING

All good love stories should have a happy ending — and the **Blind Date Book of Romance** is no exception, as we bring you a report on two Blind Daters who really did hit it off.

Karen and Alan

Him On a kissing and cuddling scale of one to ten I'd give her ten plus.

Her On a scale of one to ten as far as kissing and cuddling goes I'd give him eleven

Is this romance on the road? A perfect ending for a Blind Date.

Just a smooch at sunset, a happy ending for two of our Blind Daters at least . . .

IF YOU THINK YOU HAVE
WHAT IT TAKES TO BE
A BLIND DATE CONTESTANT
THEN WRITE FOR AN
APPLICATION FORM TO:

BLIND DATE PRODUCTION OFFICE
LONDON WEEKEND TELEVISION LIMITED
SOUTH BANK TELEVISION CENTRE
LONDON SE1 9LT